대한민국 헌법

대한민국은 민주공화국이다

대한민국 민국 헌법

대한민국 지음

더휴먼

차 례

책을 내면서 … 6

제1부
대한민국 헌법

전문 … 11

제1장 **총강** … 15

제2장 **국민의 권리와 의무** … 19

제3장 **국회** … 33

제4장 **정부** … 44

제5장 **법원** … 59

제6장 **헌법재판소** … 64

제7장 **선거관리** … 67

제8장 **지방자치** … 70

제9장 **경제** … 72

제10장 **헌법개정** … 76

부칙 … 78

제 2 부

CONSTITUTION OF REPUBLIC OF KOREA

PREAMBLE ⋯ 83

Chapter I **GENERAL PROVISIONS** ⋯ 85

Chapter II **RIGHTS AND DUTIES OF CITIZENS** ⋯ 89

Chapter III **THE NATIONAL ASSEMBLY** ⋯ 107

Chapter IV **THE EXECUTIVE** ⋯ 123

Chapter V **THE COURTS** ⋯ 144

Chapter VI **THE CONSTITUTIONAL COURT** ⋯ 151

Chapter VII **ELECTION MANAGEMENT** ⋯ 155

Chapter VIII **LOCAL AUTONOMY** ⋯ 159

Chapter IX **THE ECONOMY** ⋯ 161

Chapter X **AMENDMENTS TO THE CONSTITUTION** ⋯ 167

ADDENDA ⋯ 170

"대한민국은 민주공화국이다."

헌법 제1장 1조다. 그런데 과연 대한민국은 민주공화국일까? 주권은 국민에게 있고 권력은 국민으로부터 나올까? 한때 대한민국은 아시아 민주주의의 모범국이었다. 그러나 군사독재로 인해 인권후진국이라는 오명을 쓴 적도 있었다. 그럼에도 대한민국 헌법은 선거를 통한 평화로운 정권 교체, 부정부패를 단죄하는 삼권분립제도, 촛불혁명으로 표출된 민의를 기점으로 나날이 발전하고 있고, 코로나19라는 전 세계적인 위기 속에서도 성숙

해진 시민의식을 통해 민주주의는 2021년의 대한민국이 민주공화국임을 다시금 상기시켜 주고 있다.

법이란 개인과 개인이 만나서 사회와 국가를 만들고 더불어 살아가기 위해 세운 기준이다. 그중에서도 헌법은 모든 법의 근거이자 뿌리로, 법 중의 법이며 국민의 기본권을 보장하고 국가의 정체성을 밝힌다. 그리고 국가는 헌법 아래 모든 것을 집행할 의무가 있다. 하지만 이것이 제대로 지켜지지 않기 때문에 사회가 무너지고 인간성이 사라지며 폭력과 차별, 억압이 난무하는 것이다. 이런 사회에서 벗어나려면 헌법대로 살고 헌법대로인 나라를 만들어야 한다.

그런데 우리 중에 헌법을 처음부터 끝까지 읽은 사람이 몇이나 될까? 아주 단편적으로 집회·결사의 자유가 있고 권력은 국민으로부터 나온다 등만 알 뿐 대부분은 제대로 읽어보지도, 전문을 가지고 있지도 않다. 소위 통치자니 권력자니 하는 이들은 말로는 국민을 위해 일한다고 하지만 사실 국민의 주인으로 군림했지 일꾼이었던 적은 없었다. 헌법이 보장한 권력의 주인 자리를 찾고 존엄성을 가진 인간으로 대우받고 살아가려면 헌법부터 읽어야 한다. 모든 것의 뿌리이며 문제 해결의 열쇠이자 비판의 근거 그리고 나아갈 방향을 가리키는 이정표인 헌법을 읽지 않고는 아무것도 할 수 없다. 이제 당신의 권리와 민주주의, 존엄성을 찾으려면 헌법 읽기부터 시작해야 한다.

편집자주

"국가? 증인이 말하는 국가는 대체 뭡니까?"
"변호사라는 사람이 국가가 뭔지 몰라?"
"압니다. 너무 잘 알지요. 대한민국 헌법 제1조 2항. 대한민국 주권은 국민에 있고 모든 권력은 국민으로부터 나온다. 국가란 국민입니다!"

_영화 〈변호인〉 중에서

제 1 부

대한민국 헌법

전문

유구한 역사와 전통에 빛나는 우리 대한국민은 3·1운동으로 건립된 대한민국임시정부의 법통과 불의에 항거한 4·19민주이념을 계승하고, 조국의 민주개혁과 평화적 통일의 사명에 입각하여 정의·인도와 동포애로써 민족의 단결을 공고히 하고, 모든 사회적 폐습과 불의를 타파하며, 자율과 조화를 바탕으로 자유민주적 기본질서를 더욱 확고히 하여 정치·경제·사회·문화의 모든 영역에 있어서 각인의 기회를 균등히 하고, 능력을 최고도로 발휘하게 하며, 자유와 권리에 따르는 책임과 의무를 완수하게 하여, 안으로는 국민생활의 균등한 향상을 기하고 밖으로는 항구적인 세계평화와 인류공영에 이바지함으로써 우리들과 우리들의 자손의 안전과 자유와 행복을 영원히 확보할 것을 다짐하면서 1948년 7월 12일에 제정되고 8차에 걸쳐 개정된 헌법을 이제 국회의 의결을 거쳐 국민투표에 의하여 개정한다.

[헌법 제10호 1987.10.29. 전부 개정 / 시행 1988.2.25.]

대한민국헌법

공포	1948. 7. 17.
개정	1952. 7. 7.
	1954. 11. 29.
	1960. 6. 15.
	1960. 11. 29.
	1962. 12. 26. (전문 개정)
	1969. 10. 21.
	1972. 12. 27. (전문 개정)
	1980. 10. 27. (전문 개정)
	1987. 10. 29. (전문 개정)

제1장

총강

제1조

① 대한민국은 민주공화국이다.

② 대한민국의 주권은 국민에게 있고, 모든 권력은 국민으로부터 나온다.

제2조

① 대한민국의 국민이 되는 요건은 법률로 정한다.

② 국가는 법률이 정하는 바에 의하여 재외국민을 보호할 의무를 진다.

제3조

대한민국의 영토는 한반도와 그 부속도서로 한다.

제4조

대한민국은 통일을 지향하며, 자유민주적 기본질서에 입각한 평화적 통일정책을 수립하고 이를 추진한다.

제5조

① 대한민국은 국제평화의 유지에 노력하고 침략적 전쟁을 부인한다.

② 국군은 국가의 안전보장과 국토방위의 신성한 의무를 수행함을 사명으로 하며, 그 정치적 중립성은 준수된다.

제6조

① 헌법에 의하여 체결·공포된 조약과 일반적으로 승인된 국제법규는 국내법과 같은 효력을 가진다.

② 외국인은 국제법과 조약이 정하는 바에 의하여 그 지위가 보장된다.

제7조

① 공무원은 국민전체에 대한 봉사자이며, 국민에 대하여 책임을 진다.

② 공무원의 신분과 정치적 중립성은 법률이 정하는 바에 의하여 보장된다.

제8조

① 정당의 설립은 자유이며, 복수정당제는 보장된다.

② 정당은 그 목적, 조직과 활동이 민주적이어야 하며, 국민의 정치적 의사형성에 참여하는 데 필요한 조직을 가져야 한다.

③ 정당은 법률이 정하는 바에 의하여 국가의 보호를 받으며, 국가는 법률이 정하는 바에 의하여 정당운영에 필요한 자금을 보조할 수 있다.

④ 정당의 목적이나 활동이 민주적 기본질서에 위배될 때에는 정부는 헌법재판소에 그 해산을 제소할 수 있고, 정당은 헌법재판소의 심판에 의하여 해산된다.

제9조

국가는 전통문화의 계승·발전과 민족문화의 창달에
노력하여야 한다.

제2장

국민의 권리와 의무

제10조

모든 국민은 인간으로서의 존엄과 가치를 가지며, 행복을 추구할 권리를 가진다. 국가는 개인이 가지는 불가침의 기본적 인권을 확인하고 이를 보장할 의무를 진다.

제11조

① 모든 국민은 법 앞에 평등하다. 누구든지 성별·종교 또는 사회적 신분에 의하여 정치적·경제적·사회적·문화적 생활의 모든 영역에 있어서 차별을 받

지 아니한다.

② 사회적 특수계급의 제도는 인정되지 아니하며, 어떠한 형태로도 이를 창설할 수 없다.

③ 훈장 등의 영전은 이를 받은 자에게만 효력이 있고, 어떠한 특권도 이에 따르지 아니한다.

제12조

① 모든 국민은 신체의 자유를 가진다. 누구든지 법률에 의하지 아니하고는 체포, 구속, 압수, 수색 또는 심문을 받지 아니하며, 법률과 적법한 절차에 의하지 아니하고는 처벌·보안처분 또는 강제노역을 받지 아니한다.

② 모든 국민은 고문을 받지 아니하며, 형사상 자기에게 불리한 진술을 강요당하지 아니한다.

③ 체포·구속·압수 또는 수색을 할 때에는 적법한 절차에 따라 검사의 신청에 의하여 법관이 발부한 영장을 제시하여야 한다. 다만, 현행범인인 경우와 장기 3년 이상의 형에 해당하는 죄를 범하고 도피 또는 는 증거인멸의 염려가 있을 때에는 사후에 영장을

청구할 수 있다.

④ 누구든지 체포 또는 구속을 당한 때에는 즉시 변호
인의 조력을 받을 권리를 가진다. 다만, 형사피고인
이 스스로 변호인을 구할 수 없을 때에는 법률이 정
하는 바에 의하여 국가가 변호인을 붙인다.

⑤ 누구든지 체포 또는 구속의 이유와 변호인의 조력
을 받을 권리가 있음을 고지받지 아니하고는 체포
또는 구속을 당하지 아니한다. 체포 또는 구속을 당
한 자의 가족 등 법률이 정하는 자에게는 그 이유와
일시, 장소가 지체 없이 통지되어야 한다.

⑥ 누구든지 체포 또는 구속을 당한 때에는 적부의 심
사를 법원에 청구할 권리를 가진다.

⑦ 피고인의 자백이 고문·폭행·협박·구속의 부당한
장기화 또는 기망 기타의 방법에 의하여 자의로 진
술된 것이 아니라고 인정될 때 또는 정식재판에 있
어서 피고인의 자백이 그에게 불리한 유일한 증거
일 때에는 이를 유죄의 증거로 삼거나 이를 이유로
처벌할 수 없다.

제13조

① 모든 국민은 행위시의 법률에 의하여 범죄를 구성하지 아니하는 행위로 소추되지 아니하며, 동일한 범죄에 대하여 거듭 처벌받지 아니한다.

② 모든 국민은 소급입법에 의하여 참정권의 제한을 받거나 재산권을 박탈당하지 아니한다.

③ 모든 국민은 자기의 행위가 아닌 친족의 행위로 인하여 불이익한 처우를 받지 아니한다.

제14조

모든 국민은 거주 이전의 자유를 가진다.

제15조

모든 국민은 직업선택의 자유를 가진다.

제16조

모든 국민은 주거의 자유를 침해받지 아니한다. 주거에 대한 압수나 수색을 할 때에는 검사의 신청에 의하여 법관이 발부한 영장을 제시하여야 한다.

제17조

모든 국민은 사생활의 비밀과 자유를 침해받지 아니한다.

제18조

모든 국민은 통신의 비밀을 침해받지 아니한다.

제19조

모든 국민은 양심의 자유를 가진다.

제20조

① 모든 국민은 종교의 자유를 가진다.

② 국교는 인정되지 아니하며, 종교와 정치는 분리된다.

제21조

① 모든 국민은 언론·출판의 자유와 집회·결사의 자유를 가진다.

② 언론·출판에 대한 허가나 검열과 집회·결사에 대한 허가는 인정되지 아니한다.

③ 통신·방송의 시설기준과 신문의 기능을 보장하기 위하여 필요한 사항은 법률로 정한다.

④ 언론·출판은 타인의 명예나 권리 또는 공중도덕이나 사회윤리를 침해하여서는 아니된다. 언론·출판이 타인의 명예나 권리를 침해한 때에는 피해자는 이에 대한 피해의 배상을 청구할 수 있다.

제22조

① 모든 국민은 학문과 예술의 자유를 가진다.

② 저작자·발명가·과학기술자와 예술가의 권리는 법률로써 보호한다.

제23조

① 모든 국민의 재산권은 보장된다. 그 내용과 한계는 법률로 정한다.

② 재산권의 행사는 공공복리에 적합하도록 하여야 한다.

③ 공공필요에 의한 재산권의 수용, 사용 또는 제한 및 그에 대한 보상은 법률로써 하되, 정당한 보상을 지

급하여야 한다.

제24조

모든 국민은 법률이 정하는 바에 의하여 선거권을 가진다.

제25조

모든 국민은 법률이 정하는 바에 의하여 공무담임권을 가진다.

제26조

① 모든 국민은 법률이 정하는 바에 의하여 국가기관에 문서로 청원할 권리를 가진다.

② 국가는 청원에 대하여 심사할 의무를 진다.

제27조

① 모든 국민은 헌법과 법률이 정한 법관에 의하여 법률에 의한 재판을 받을 권리를 가진다.

② 군인 또는 군무원이 아닌 국민은 대한민국의 영역

안에서는 중대한 군사상 기밀, 초병, 초소, 유독음식
물공급, 포로, 군용물에 관한 죄 중 법률이 정한 경
우와 비상계엄이 선포된 경우를 제외하고는 군사
법원의 재판을 받지 아니한다.

③ 모든 국민은 신속한 재판을 받을 권리를 가진다. 형
사피고인은 상당한 이유가 없는 한 지체 없이 공개
재판을 받을 권리를 가진다.

④ 형사피고인은 유죄의 판결이 확정될 때까지는 무죄
로 추정된다.

⑤ 형사피해자는 법률이 정하는 바에 의하여 당해 사
건의 재판절차에서 진술할 수 있다.

제28조

형사피의자 또는 형사피고인으로서 구금되었던 자가
법률이 정하는 불기소처분을 받거나 무죄판결을 받은 때
에는 법률이 정하는 바에 익하여 국가에 정당한 보상을
청구할 수 있다.

제29조

① 공무원의 직무상 불법행위로 손해를 받은 국민은 법률이 정하는 바에 의하여 국가 또는 공공단체에 정당한 배상을 청구할 수 있다. 이 경우 공무원 자신의 책임은 면제되지 아니한다.

② 군인·군무원·경찰공무원 기타 법률이 정하는 자가 전투·훈련 등 직무집행과 관련하여 받은 손해에 대하여는 법률이 정하는 보상 외에 국가 또는 공공단체에 공무원의 직무상 불법행위로 인한 배상은 청구할 수 없다.

제30조

타인의 범죄행위로 인하여 생명·신체에 대한 피해를 받은 국민은 법률이 정하는 바에 의하여 국가로부터 구조를 받을 수 있다.

제31조

① 모든 국민은 능력에 따라 균등하게 교육을 받을 권리를 가진다.

② 모든 국민은 그 보호하는 자녀에게 적어도 초등교
육과 법률이 정하는 교육을 받게 할 의무를 진다.

③ 의무교육은 무상으로 한다.

④ 교육의 자주성·전문성·정치적 중립성 및 대학의
자율성은 법률이 정하는 바에 의하여 보장된다.

⑤ 국가는 평생교육을 진흥하여야 한다.

⑥ 학교교육 및 평생교육을 포함한 교육제도와 그 운
영, 교육재정 및 교원의 지위에 관한 기본적인 사항
은 법률로 정한다.

제32조

① 모든 국민은 근로의 권리를 가진다. 국가는 사회적
·경제적 방법으로 근로자의 고용의 증진과 적정임
금의 보장에 노력하여야 하며, 법률이 정하는 바에
의하여 최저임금제를 시행하여야 한다.

② 모든 국민은 근로의 의무를 진다. 국가는 근로의 의
무의 내용과 조건을 민주주의 원칙에 따라 법률로
정한다.

③ 근로조건의 기준은 인간의 존엄성을 보장하도록 법

률로 정한다.

④ 여자의 근로는 특별한 보호를 받으며, 고용·임금 및 근로조건에 있어서 부당한 차별을 받지 아니한다.

⑤ 연소자의 근로는 특별한 보호를 받는다.

⑥ 국가유공자·상이군경 및 전몰군경의 유가족은 법률이 정하는 바에 의하여 우선적으로 근로의 기회를 부여받는다.

제33조

① 근로자는 근로조건의 향상을 위하여 자주적인 단결권·단체교섭권 및 단체행동권을 가진다.

② 공무원인 근로자는 법률이 정하는 자에 한하여 단결권·단체교섭권 및 단체행동권을 가진다.

③ 법률이 정하는 주요방위산업체에 종사하는 근로자의 단체행동권은 법률이 정하는 바에 의하여 이를 제한하거나 인정하지 아니할 수 있다.

제34조

① 모든 국민은 인간다운 생활을 할 권리를 가진다.

② 국가는 사회보장·사회복지의 증진에 노력할 의무를 진다.

③ 국가는 여자의 복지와 권익의 향상을 위하여 노력하여야 한다.

④ 국가는 노인과 청소년의 복지향상을 위한 정책을 실시할 의무를 진다.

⑤ 신체장애자 및 질병·노령 기타의 사유로 생활능력이 없는 국민은 법률이 정하는 바에 의하여 국가의 보호를 받는다.

⑥ 국가는 재해를 예방하고 그 위험으로부터 국민을 보호하기 위하여 노력하여야 한다.

제35조

① 모든 국민은 건강하고 쾌적한 환경에서 생활할 권리를 가지며, 국가와 국민은 환경보전을 위하여 노력하여야 한다.

② 환경권의 내용과 행사에 관하여는 법률로 정한다.

③ 국가는 주택개발정책 등을 통하여 모든 국민이 쾌적한 주거생활을 할 수 있도록 노력하여야 한다.

제36조

① 혼인과 가족생활은 개인의 존엄과 양성의 평등을 기초로 성립되고 유지되어야 하며, 국가는 이를 보장한다.
② 국가는 모성의 보호를 위하여 노력하여야 한다.
③ 모든 국민은 보건에 관하여 국가의 보호를 받는다.

제37조

① 국민의 자유와 권리는 헌법에 열거되지 아니한 이유로 경시되지 아니한다.
② 국민의 모든 자유와 권리는 국가안전보장, 질서유지 또는 공공복리를 위하여 필요한 경우에 한하여 법률로써 제한할 수 있으며, 제한하는 경우에도 자유와 권리의 본질적인 내용을 침해할 수 없다.

제38조

　모든 국민은 법률이 정하는 바에 의하여 납세의 의무를 진다.

제39조

① 모든 국민은 법률이 정하는 바에 의하여 국방의 의무를 진다.

② 누구든지 병역의무의 이행으로 인하여 불이익한 처우를 받지 아니한다.

제3장

국회

제40조

입법권은 국회에 속한다.

제41조

① 국회는 국민의 보통·평등·직접·비밀선거에 의하여 선출된 국회의원으로 구성한다.

② 국회의원의 수는 법률로 정하되, 200인 이상으로 한다.

③ 국회의원의 선거구와 비례대표제 기타 선거에 관한

사항은 법률로 정한다.

제42조

국회의원의 임기는 4년으로 한다.

제43조

국회의원은 법률이 정하는 직을 겸할 수 없다.

제44조

① 국회의원은 현행범인 경우를 제외하고는 회기 중 국회의 동의 없이 체포 또는 구금되지 아니한다.

② 국회의원이 회기 전에 체포 또는 구금된 때에는 현행범이 아닌 한 국회의 요구가 있으면 회기 중 석방된다.

제45조

국회의원은 국회에서 직무상 행한 발언과 표결에 관하여 국회 외에서 책임을 지지 아니한다.

제46조

① 국회의원은 청렴의 의무가 있다.

② 국회의원은 국가이익을 우선하여 양심에 따라 직무를 행한다.

③ 국회의원은 그 지위를 남용하여 국가·공공단체 또는 기업체와의 계약이나 그 처분에 의하여 재산상의 권리·이익 또는 직위를 취득하거나 타인을 위하여 그 취득을 알선할 수 없다.

제47조

① 국회의 정기회는 법률이 정하는 바에 의하여 매년 1회 집회되며, 국회의 임시회는 대통령 또는 국회재적의원 4분의 1 이상의 요구에 의하여 집회된다.

② 정기회의 회기는 100일을, 임시회의 회기는 30일을 초과할 수 없다.

③ 대통령이 임시회의 집회를 요구할 때에는 기간과 집회 요구의 이유를 명시하여야 한다.

제48조

국회는 의장 1인과 부의장 2인을 선출한다.

제49조

국회는 헌법 또는 법률에 특별한 규정이 없는 한 재적의원 과반수의 출석과 출석의원 과반수의 찬성으로 의결한다. 가부동수인 때에는 부결된 것으로 본다.

제50조

① 국회의 회의는 공개한다. 다만, 출석의원 과반수의 찬성이 있거나 의장이 국가의 안전보장을 위하여 필요하다고 인정할 때에는 공개하지 아니할 수 있다.
② 공개하지 아니한 회의내용의 공표에 관하여는 법률이 정하는 바에 의한다.

제51조

국회에 제출된 법률안 기타의 의안은 회기 중에 의결되지 못한 이유로 폐기되지 아니한다. 다만, 국회의원의 임기가 만료된 때에는 그러하지 아니한다.

제52조

국회의원과 정부는 법률안을 제출할 수 있다.

제53조

① 국회에서 의결된 법률안은 정부에 이송되어 15일 이내에 대통령이 공포한다.

② 법률안에 이의가 있을 때에는 대통령은 제1항의 기간 내에 이의서를 붙여 국회로 환부하고, 그 재의를 요구할 수 있다. 국회의 폐회 중에도 또한 같다.

③ 대통령은 법률안의 일부에 대하여 또는 법률안을 수정하여 재의를 요구할 수 없다.

④ 재의의 요구가 있을 때에는 국회는 재의에 붙이고, 재적의원 과반수의 출석과 출석의원 3분의 2 이상의 찬성으로 전과 같은 의결을 하면 그 법률안은 법률로서 확정된다.

⑤ 대통령이 제1항의 기간 내에 공포나 재의의 요구를 하지 아니한 때에도 그 법률안은 법률로서 확정된다.

⑥ 대통령은 제4항과 제5항의 규정에 의하여 확정된

법률을 지체 없이 공포하여야 한다. 제5항에 의하여 법률이 확정된 후 또는 제4항에 의한 확정법률이 정부에 이송된 후 5일 이내에 대통령이 공포하지 아니할 때에는 국회의장이 이를 공포한다.

⑦ 법률은 특별한 규정이 없는 한 공포한 날로부터 20일을 경과함으로써 효력을 발생한다.

제54조

① 국회는 국가의 예산안을 심의·확정한다.

② 정부는 회계연도마다 예산안을 편성하여 회계연도 개시 90일 전까지 국회에 제출하고, 국회는 회계연도 개시 30일 전까지 이를 의결하여야 한다.

③ 새로운 회계연도가 개시될 때까지 예산안이 의결되지 못한 때에는 정부는 국회에서 예산안이 의결될 때까지 다음의 목적을 위한 경비는 전년도 예산에 준하여 집행할 수 있다.

1. 헌법이나 법률에 의하여 설치된 기관 또는 시설의 유지·운영

2. 법률상 지출의무의 이행

3. 이미 예산으로 승인된 사업의 계속

제55조

① 한 회계연도를 넘어 계속하여 지출할 필요가 있을 때에는 정부는 연한을 정하여 계속비로서 국회의 의결을 얻어야 한다.

② 예비비는 총액으로 국회의 의결을 얻어야 한다. 예비비의 지출은 차기국회의 승인을 얻어야 한다.

제56조

정부는 예산에 변경을 가할 필요가 있을 때에는 추가경정 예산안을 편성하여 국회에 제출할 수 있다.

제57조

국회는 정부의 동의 없이 정부가 제출한 지출예산 각 항의 금액을 증가하거나 새 비목을 설치할 수 없다.

제58조

국채를 모집하거나 예산외에 국가의 부담이 될 계약을

체결하려 할 때에는 정부는 미리 국회의 의결을 얻어야 한다.

제59조

조세의 종목과 세율은 법률로 정한다.

제60조

① 국회는 상호원조 또는 안전보장에 관한 조약, 중요한 국제조직에 관한 조약, 우호통상항해조약, 주권의 제약에 관한 조약, 강화조약, 국가나 국민에게 중대한 재정적 부담을 지우는 조약 또는 입법사항에 관한 조약의 체결·비준에 대한 동의권을 가진다.

② 국회는 선전포고, 국군의 외국에의 파견 또는 외국군대의 대한민국 영역 안에서의 주류에 대한 동의권을 가진다.

제61조

① 국회는 국정을 감사하거나 특정한 국정사안에 대하여 조사할 수 있으며, 이에 필요한 서류의 제출 또

는 증인의 출석과 증언이나 의견의 진술을 요구할
수 있다.

② 국정감사 및 조사에 관한 절차 기타 필요한 사항은
법률로 정한다.

제62조

① 국무총리·국무위원 또는 정부위원은 국회나 그 위
원회에 출석하여 국정처리상황을 보고하거나 의견
을 진술하고 질문에 응답할 수 있다.

② 국회나 그 위원회의 요구가 있을 때에는 국무총리·
국무위원 또는 정부위원은 출석·답변하여야 하며,
국무총리 또는 국무위원이 출석요구를 받은 때에
는 국무위원 또는 정부위원으로 하여금 출석·답변
하게 할 수 있다.

제63조

① 국회는 국무총리 또는 국무위원의 해임을 대통령에
게 건의할 수 있다.

② 제1항의 해임건의는 국회재적의원 3분의 1 이상의

발의에 의하여 국회재적의원 과반수의 찬성이 있
어야 한다.

제64조

① 국회는 법률에 저촉되지 아니하는 범위 안에서 의
사와 내부규율에 관한 규칙을 제정할 수 있다.

② 국회는 의원의 자격을 심사하며, 의원을 징계할 수
있다.

③ 의원을 제명하려면 국회재적의원 3분의 2 이상의
찬성이 있어야 한다.

④ 제2항과 제3항의 처분에 대하여는 법원에 제소할
수 없다.

제65조

① 대통령·국무총리·국무위원·행정각부의 장·헌법
재판소 재판관·법관·중앙선거관리위원회 위원·감
사원장·감사위원 기타 법률이 정한 공무원이 그 직
무집행에 있어서 헌법이나 법률을 위배한 때에는
국회는 탄핵의 소추를 의결할 수 있다.

② 제1항의 탄핵소추는 국회재적의원 3분의 1 이상의 발의가 있어야 하며, 그 의결은 국회재적의원 과반수의 찬성이 있어야 한다. 다만, 대통령에 대한 탄핵소추는 국회재적의원 과반수의 발의와 국회재적의원 3분의 2 이상의 찬성이 있어야 한다.

③ 탄핵소추의 의결을 받은 자는 탄핵심판이 있을 때까지 그 권한행사가 정지된다.

④ 탄핵결정은 공직으로부터 파면함에 그친다. 그러나 이에 의하여 민사상이나 형사상의 책임이 면제되지는 아니한다.

제4장

정부

제1절 대통령

제66조

① 대통령은 국가의 원수이며, 외국에 대하여 국가를 대표한다.

② 대통령은 국가의 독립·영토의 보전·국가의 계속성과 헌법을 수호할 책무를 진다.

③ 대통령은 조국의 평화적 통일을 위한 성실한 의무를 진다.

④ 행정권은 대통령을 수반으로 하는 정부에 속한다.

제67조

① 대통령은 국민의 보통·평등·직접·비밀선거에 의하여 선출한다.

② 제1항의 선거에 있어서 최고득표자가 2인 이상인 때에는 국회의 재적의원 과반수가 출석한 공개회의에서 다수표를 얻은 자를 당선자로 한다.

③ 대통령후보자가 1인일 때에는 그 득표수가 선거권자 총수의 3분의 1 이상이 아니면 대통령으로 당선될 수 없다.

④ 대통령으로 선거될 수 있는 자는 국회의원의 피선거권이 있고 선거일 현재 40세에 달하여야 한다.

⑤ 대통령의 선거에 관한 사항은 법률로 정한다.

제68조

① 대통령의 임기가 만료되는 때에는 임기만료 70일 내지 40일 전에 후임자를 선거한다.

② 대통령이 궐위된 때 또는 대통령 당선자가 사망하

거나 판결 기타의 사유로 그 자격을 상실한 때에는 60일 이내에 후임자를 선거한다.

제69조

대통령은 취임에 즈음하여 다음의 선서를 한다. "나는 헌법을 준수하고 국가를 보위하며 조국의 평화적 통일과 국민의 자유와 복리의 증진 및 민족문화의 창달에 노력하여 대통령으로서의 직책을 성실히 수행할 것을 국민 앞에 엄숙히 선서합니다."

제70조

대통령의 임기는 5년으로 하며, 중임할 수 없다.

제71조

대통령이 궐위되거나 사고로 인하여 직무를 수행할 수 없을 때에는 국무총리, 법률이 정한 국무위원의 순서로 그 권한을 대행한다.

제72조

대통령은 필요하다고 인정할 때에는 외교·국방·통일 기타 국가안위에 관한 중요정책을 국민투표에 붙일 수 있다.

제73조

대통령은 조약을 체결·비준하고, 외교사절을 신임·접수 또는 파견하며, 선전포고와 강화를 한다.

제74조

① 대통령은 헌법과 법률이 정하는 바에 의하여 국군을 통수한다.

② 국군의 조직과 편성은 법률로 정한다.

제75조

대통령은 법률에서 구체적으로 범위를 정하여 위임받은 사항과 법률을 집행하기 위하여 필요한 사항에 관하여 대통령령을 발할 수 있다.

제76조

① 대통령은 내우·외환·천재·지변 또는 중대한 재정·경제상의 위기에 있어서 국가의 안전보장 또는 공공의 안녕질서를 유지하기 위하여 긴급한 조치가 필요하고 국회의 집회를 기다릴 여유가 없을 때에 한하여 최소한으로 필요한 재정·경제상의 처분을 하거나 이에 관하여 법률의 효력을 가지는 명령을 발할 수 있다.

② 대통령은 국가의 안위에 관계되는 중대한 교전상태에 있어서 국가를 보위하기 위하여 긴급한 조치가 필요하고 국회의 집회가 불가능한 때에 한하여 법률의 효력을 가지는 명령을 발할 수 있다.

③ 대통령은 제1항과 제2항의 처분 또는 명령을 한 때에는 지체 없이 국회에 보고하여 그 승인을 얻어야 한다.

④ 제3항의 승인을 얻지 못한 때에는 그 처분 또는 명령은 그때부터 효력을 상실한다. 이 경우 그 명령에 의하여 개정 또는 폐지되었던 법률은 그 명령이 승인을 얻지 못한 때부터 당연히 효력을 회복한다.

⑤ 대통령은 제3항과 제4항의 사유를 지체 없이 공포
하여야 한다.

제77조

① 대통령은 전시·사변 또는 이에 준하는 국가비상사
태에 있어서 병력으로써 군사상의 필요에 응하거
나 공공의 안녕질서를 유지할 필요가 있을 때에는
법률이 정하는 바에 의하여 계엄을 선포할 수 있다.

② 계엄은 비상계엄과 경비계엄으로 한다.

③ 비상계엄이 선포된 때에는 법률이 정하는 바에 의
하여 영장제도, 언론·출판·집회·결사의 자유, 정
부나 법원의 권한에 관하여 특별한 조치를 할 수
있다.

④ 계엄을 선포한 때에는 대통령은 지체 없이 국회에
통고하여야 한다.

⑤ 국회가 재적의원 과반수의 찬성으로 계엄의 해제를
요구한 때에는 대통령은 이를 해제하여야 한다.

제78조

　대통령은 헌법과 법률이 정하는 바에 의하여 공무원을 임면한다.

제79조

① 대통령은 법률이 정하는 바에 의하여 사면·감형 또는 복권을 명할 수 있다.
② 일반사면을 명하려면 국회의 동의를 얻어야 한다.
③ 사면·감형 및 복권에 관한 사항은 법률로 정한다.

제80조

　대통령은 법률이 정하는 바에 의하여 훈장 기타의 영전을 수여한다.

제81조

　대통령은 국회에 출석하여 발언하거나 서한으로 의견을 표시할 수 있다.

제82조

대통령의 국법상 행위는 문서로써 하며, 이 문서에는 국무총리와 관계 국무위원이 부서한다. 군사에 관한 것도 또한 같다.

제83조

대통령은 국무총리·국무위원·행정각부의 장 기타 법률이 정하는 공사의 직을 겸할 수 없다.

제84조

대통령은 내란 또는 외환의 죄를 범한 경우를 제외하고는 재직 중 형사상의 소추를 받지 아니한다.

제85조

전직대통령의 신분과 예우에 관하여는 법률로 정한다.

제2절 행정부

제1관 국무총리와 국무위원

제86조

① 국무총리는 국회의 동의를 얻어 대통령이 임명한다.

② 국무총리는 대통령을 보좌하며, 행정에 관하여 대통령의 명을 받아 행정각부를 통할한다.

③ 군인은 현역을 면한 후가 아니면 국무총리로 임명될 수 없다.

제87조

① 국무위원은 국무총리의 제청으로 대통령이 임명한다.

② 국무위원은 국정에 관하여 대통령을 보좌하며, 국무회의의 구성원으로서 국정을 심의한다.

③ 국무총리는 국무위원의 해임을 대통령에게 건의할 수 있다.

④ 군인은 현역을 면한 후가 아니면 국무위원으로 임

명될 수 없다.

제2관 국무회의

제88조

① 국무회의는 정부의 권한에 속하는 중요한 정책을 심의한다.

② 국무회의는 대통령·국무총리와 15인 이상 30인 이하의 국무위원으로 구성한다.

③ 대통령은 국무회의의 의장이 되고, 국무총리는 부의장이 된다.

제89조

다음 사항은 국무회의의 심의를 거쳐야 한다.

1. 국정의 기본계획과 정부의 일반정책

2. 선전·강화 기타 중요한 대외정책

3. 헌법개정안·국민투표안·조약안·법률안 및 대통령령안

4. 예산안·결산·국유재산처분의 기본계획·국가의 부담이 될 계약 기타 재정에 관한 중요사항

5. 대통령의 긴급명령·긴급재정경제처분 및 명령 또는 계엄과 그 해제

6. 군사에 관한 중요사항

7. 국회의 임시회 집회의 요구

8. 영전수여

9. 사면·감형과 복권

10. 행정각부간의 권한의 획정

11. 정부 안의 권한의 위임 또는 배정에 관한 기본계획

12. 국정처리상황의 평가·분석

13. 행정각부의 중요한 정책의 수립과 조정

14. 정당해산의 제소

15. 정부에 제출 또는 회부된 정부의 정책에 관계되는 청원의 심사

16. 검찰청장·합동참모의장·각군침모총장·국립대학교 총장·대사 기타 법률이 정한 공무원과 국영기업체 관리자의 임명

17. 기타 대통령·국무총리 또는 국무위원이 제출한

사항

제90조

① 국정의 중요한 사항에 관한 대통령의 자문에 응하기 위하여 국가원로로 구성되는 국가원로자문회의를 둘 수 있다.

② 국가원로자문회의의 의장은 직전대통령이 된다. 다만, 직전대통령이 없을 때에는 대통령이 지명한다.

③ 국가원로자문회의의 조직·직무범위 기타 필요한 사항은 법률로 정한다.

제91조

① 국가안전보장에 관련되는 대외정책·군사정책과 국내 정책의 수립에 관하여 국무회의의 심의에 앞서 대통령의 자문에 응하기 위하여 국가안전보장회의를 둔다.

② 국가안전보장회의는 대통령이 주재한다.

③ 국가안전보장회의의 조직·직무범위 기타 필요한 사항은 법률로 정한다.

제92조

① 평화통일정책의 수립에 관한 대통령의 자문에 응하기 위하여 민주평화통일 자문회의를 둘 수 있다.

② 민주평화통일자문회의의 조직·직무범위 기타 필요한 사항은 법률로 정한다.

제93조

① 국민경제의 발전을 위한 중요정책의 수립에 관하여 대통령의 자문에 응하기 위하여 국민경제자문회의를 둘 수 있다.

② 국민경제자문회의의 조직·직무범위 기타 필요한 사항은 법률로 정한다.

제3관 행정각부

제94조

행정각부의 장은 국무위원 중에서 국무총리의 제청으로 대통령이 임명한다.

제95조

국무총리 또는 행정각부의 장은 소관사무에 관하여 법률이나 대통령령의 위임 또는 직권으로 총리령 또는 부령을 발할 수 있다.

제96조

행정각부의 설치·조직과 직무범위는 법률로 정한다.

제4관 감사원

제97조

국가의 세입·세출의 결산, 국가 및 법률이 정한 단체의 회계검사와 행정기관 및 공무원의 직무에 관한 감찰을 하기 위하여 대통령 소속하에 감사원을 둔다.

제98조

① 감사원은 원장을 포함한 5인 이상 11인 이하의 감사위원으로 구성한다.

② 원장은 국회의 동의를 얻어 대통령이 임명하고, 그 임기는 4년으로 하며, 1차에 한하여 중임할 수 있다.

③ 감사위원은 원장의 제청으로 대통령이 임명하고, 그 임기는 4년으로 하며, 1차에 한하여 중임할 수 있다.

제99조

감사원은 세입·세출의 결산을 매년 검사하여 대통령과 차년도 국회에 그 결과를 보고하여야 한다.

제100조

감사원의 조직·직무범위·감사위원의 자격·감사 대상 공무원의 범위 기타 필요한 사항은 법률로 정한다.

법원

제101조

① 사법권은 법관으로 구성된 법원에 속한다.

② 법원은 최고법원인 대법원과 각급법원으로 조직된다.

③ 법관의 자격은 법률로 정한다.

제102조

① 대법원에 부를 둘 수 있다.

② 대법원에 대법관을 둔다. 다만, 법률이 정하는 바에

의하여 대법관이 아닌 법관을 둘 수 있다.

③ 대법원과 각급법원의 조직은 법률로 정한다.

제103조

법관은 헌법과 법률에 의하여 그 양심에 따라 독립하여 심판한다.

제104조

① 대법원장은 국회의 동의를 얻어 대통령이 임명한다.

② 대법관은 대법원장의 제청으로 국회의 동의를 얻어 대통령이 임명한다.

③ 대법원장과 대법관이 아닌 법관은 대법관회의의 동의를 얻어 대법원장이 임명한다.

제105조

① 대법원장의 임기는 6년으로 하며, 중임할 수 없다.

② 대법관의 임기는 6년으로 하며, 법률이 정하는 바에 의하여 연임할 수 있다.

③ 대법원장과 대법관이 아닌 법관의 임기는 10년으

로 하며, 법률이 정하는 바에 의하여 연임할 수 있다.

④ 법관의 정년은 법률로 정한다.

제106조

① 법관은 탄핵 또는 금고 이상의 형의 선고에 의하지 아니하고는 파면되지 아니하며, 징계처분에 의하지 아니하고는 정직·감봉 기타 불리한 처분을 받지 아니한다.

② 법관이 중대한 심신상의 장해로 직무를 수행할 수 없을 때에는 법률이 정하는 바에 의하여 퇴직하게 할 수 있다.

제107조

① 법률이 헌법에 위반되는 여부가 재판의 전제가 된 경우에는 법원은 헌법재판소에 제청하여 그 심판에 의하여 재판한다.

② 명령·규칙 또는 처분이 헌법이나 법률에 위반되는 여부가 재판의 전제가 된 경우에는 대법원은 이를 최종적으로 심사할 권한을 가진다.

③ 재판의 전심절차로서 행정심판을 할 수 있다. 행정
심판의 절차는 법률로 정하되, 사법절차가 준용되
어야 한다.

제108조

대법원은 법률에 저촉되지 아니하는 범위 안에서 소송
에 관한 절차, 법원의 내부규율과 사무처리에 관한 규칙
을 제정할 수 있다.

제109조

재판의 심리와 판결은 공개한다. 다만, 심리는 국가의
안전보장 또는 안녕질서를 방해하거나 선량한 풍속을 해
할 염려가 있을 때에는 법원의 결정으로 공개하지 아니
할 수 있다.

제110조

① 군사재판을 관할하기 위하여 특별법원으로서 군사
법원을 둘 수 있다.
② 군사법원의 상고심은 대법원에서 관할한다.

③ 군사법원의 조직·권한 및 재판관의 자격은 법률로
정한다.

④ 비상계엄상의 군사재판은 군인·군무원의 범죄나 군
사에 관한 간첩죄의 경우와 초병·초소·유독음식물
공급·포로에 관한 죄 중 법률이 정한 경우에 한하여
단심으로 할 수 있다. 다만, 사형을 선고한 경우에는
그러하지 아니한다.

제6장

헌법재판소

제111조

　① 헌법재판소는 다음 사항을 관장한다.

　　1. 법원의 제청에 의한 법률의 위헌여부 심판

　　2. 탄핵의 심판

　　3. 정당의 해산 심판

　　4. 국가기관 상호간, 국가기관과 지방자치단체간 및
　　　지방자치단체 상호간의 권한쟁의에 관한 심판

　　5. 법률이 정하는 헌법소원에 관한 심판

　② 헌법재판소는 법관의 자격을 가진 9인의 재판관으

로 구성하며, 재판관은 대통령이 임명한다.

③ 제2항의 재판관 중 3인은 국회에서 선출하는 자를, 3인은 대법원장이 지명하는 자를 임명한다.

④ 헌법재판소의 장은 국회의 동의를 얻어 재판관중에서 대통령이 임명한다.

제112조

① 헌법재판소 재판관의 임기는 6년으로 하며, 법률이 정하는 바에 의하여 연임할 수 있다.

② 헌법재판소 재판관은 정당에 가입하거나 정치에 관여할 수 없다.

③ 헌법재판소 재판관은 탄핵 또는 금고 이상의 형의 선고에 의하지 아니하고는 파면되지 아니한다.

제113조

① 헌법재판소에서 법률의 위헌결정, 탄핵의 결정, 정당해산의 결정 또는 헌법소원에 관한 인용결정을 할 때에는 재판관 6인 이상의 찬성이 있어야 한다.

② 헌법재판소는 법률에 저촉되지 아니하는 범위 안에

서 심판에 관한 절차, 내부규율과 사무처리에 관한 규칙을 제정할 수 있다.

③ 헌법재판소의 조직과 운영 기타 필요한 사항은 법률로 정한다.

선거관리

제114조

① 선거와 국민투표의 공정한 관리 및 정당에 관한 사무를 처리하기 위하여 선거관리위원회를 둔다.

② 중앙선거관리위원회는 대통령이 임명하는 3인, 국회에서 선출하는 3인과 대법원장이 지명하는 3인의 위원으로 구성한다. 위원장은 위원 중에서 호선한다.

③ 위원의 임기는 6년으로 한다.

④ 위원은 정당에 가입하거나 정치에 관여할 수 없다.

⑤ 위원은 탄핵 또는 금고 이상의 형의 선고에 의하지 아니하고는 파면되지 아니한다.

⑥ 중앙선거관리위원회는 법령의 범위 안에서 선거관리·국민투표관리 또는 정당사무에 관한 규칙을 제정할 수 있으며, 법률에 저촉되지 아니하는 범위 안에서 내부규율에 관한 규칙을 제정할 수 있다.

⑦ 각급 선거관리위원회의 조직·직무범위 기타 필요한 사항은 법률로 정한다.

제115조

① 각급 선거관리위원회는 선거인명부의 작성 등 선거사무와 국민투표사무에 관하여 관계 행정기관에 필요한 지시를 할 수 있다.

② 제1항의 지시를 받은 당해 행정기관은 이에 응하여야 한다.

제116조

① 선거운동은 각급 선거관리위원회의 관리하에 법률이 정하는 범위 안에서 하되, 균등한 기회가 보장되

어야 한다.

② 선거에 관한 경비는 법률이 정하는 경우를 제외하
고는 정당 또는 후보자에게 부담시킬 수 없다.

제8장

지방자치

제117조

① 지방자치단체는 주민의 복리에 관한 사무를 처리하고 재산을 관리하며, 법령의 범위 안에서 자치에 관한 규정을 제정할 수 있다.

② 지방자치단체의 종류는 법률로 정한다.

제118조

① 지방자치단체에 의회를 둔다.

② 지방의회의 조직·권한·의원선거와 지방자치단체

의장의 선임방법 기타 지방자치 단체의 조직과 운영에 관한 사항은 법률로 정한다.

경제

제119조

① 대한민국의 경제질서는 개인과 기업의 경제상의 자유와 창의를 존중함을 기본으로 한다.

② 국가는 균형 있는 국민경제의 성장 및 안정과 적정한 소득의 분배를 유지하고, 시장의 지배와 경제력의 남용을 방지하며, 경제주체간의 조화를 통한 경제의 민주화를 위하여 경제에 관한 규제와 조정을 할 수 있다.

제120조

① 광물 기타 중요한 지하자원·수산자원·수력과 경제상 이용할 수 있는 자연력은 법률이 정하는 바에 의하여 일정한 기간 그 채취·개발 또는 이용을 특허할 수 있다.

② 국토와 자원은 국가의 보호를 받으며, 국가는 그 균형있는 개발과 이용을 위하여 필요한 계획을 수립한다.

제121조

① 국가는 농지에 관하여 경자유전의 원칙이 달성될 수 있도록 노력하여야 하며, 농지의 소작제도는 금지된다.

② 농업생산성의 제고와 농지의 합리적인 이용을 위하거나 불가피한 사정으로 발생하는 농지의 임대차와 위탁 경영은 법률이 정하는 바에 의하여 인정된다.

제122조

국가는 국민 모두의 생산 및 생활의 기반이 되는 국토

의 효율적이고 균형 있는 이용·개발과 보전을 위하여 법률이 정하는 바에 의하여 그에 관한 필요한 제한과 의무를 과할 수 있다.

제123조

① 국가는 농업 및 어업을 보호·육성하기 위하여 농·어촌종합개발과 그 지원 등 필요한 계획을 수립·시행하여야 한다.

② 국가는 지역간의 균형 있는 발전을 위하여 지역경제를 육성할 의무를 진다.

③ 국가는 중소기업을 보호·육성하여야 한다.

④ 국가는 농수산물의 수급균형과 유통구조의 개선에 노력하여 가격안정을 도모함으로써 농·어민의 이익을 보호한다.

⑤ 국가는 농·어민과 중소기업의 자조조직을 육성하여야 하며, 그 자율적 활동과 발전을 보상한다.

제124조

국가는 건전한 소비행위를 계도하고 생산품의 품질향

상을 촉구하기 위한 소비자보호운동을 법률이 정하는 바에 의하여 보장한다.

제125조

국가는 대외무역을 육성하며, 이를 규제·조정할 수 있다.

제126조

국방상 또는 국민경제상 긴절한 필요로 인하여 법률이 정하는 경우를 제외하고는, 사영기업을 국유 또는 공유로 이전하거나 그 경영을 통제 또는 관리 할 수 없다.

제127조

① 국가는 과학기술의 혁신과 정보 및 인력의 개발을 통하여 국민경제의 발전에 노력하여야 한다.

② 국가는 국가표준제도를 확립한다.

③ 대통령은 제1항의 목적을 달성하기 위하여 필요한 자문기구를 둘 수 있다.

제10장

헌법개정

제128조

① 헌법개정은 국회재적의원 과반수 또는 대통령의 발의로 제안된다.

② 대통령의 임기연장 또는 중임변경을 위한 헌법개정은 그 헌법개정 제안 당시의 대통령에 대하여는 효력이 없다.

제129조

제안된 헌법개정안은 대통령이 20일 이상의 기간 이를

공고하여야 한다.

제130조

① 국회는 헌법개정안이 공고된 날로부터 60일 이내
   에 의결하여야 하며, 국회의 의결은 재적의원 3분
   의 2 이상의 찬성을 얻어야 한다.

② 헌법개정안은 국회가 의결한 후 30일 이내에 국민
   투표에 붙여 국회의원 선거권자 과반수의 투표와
   투표자 과반수의 찬성을 얻어야 한다.

③ 헌법개정안이 제2항의 찬성을 얻은 때에는 헌법
   개정은 확정되며, 대통령은 즉시 이를 공포하여야
   한다.

부칙

제1조

이 헌법은 1988년 2월 25일부터 시행한다. 다만, 이 헌법을 시행하기 위하여 필요한 법률의 제정·개정과 이 헌법에 의한 대통령 및 국회의원의 선거 기타 이 헌법시행에 관한 준비는 이 헌법시행 전에 할 수 있다.

제2조

① 이 헌법에 의한 최초의 대통령선거는 이 헌법시행일 40일 전까지 실시한다.

② 이 헌법에 의한 최초의 대통령의 임기는 이 헌법시
행일로부터 개시한다.

제3조

① 이 헌법에 의한 최초의 국회의원선거는 이 헌법공
포일로부터 6월 이내에 실시하며, 이 헌법에 의하
여 선출된 최초의 국회의원의 임기는 국회의원선
거 후 이 헌법에 의한 국회의 최초의 집회일로부터
개시한다.

② 이 헌법공포 당시의 국회의원의 임기는 제1항에 의
한 국회의 최초의 집회일 전일까지로 한다.

제4조

① 이 헌법시행 당시의 공무원과 정부가 임명한 기업
체의 임원은 이 헌법에 의하여 임명된 것으로 본다.
다만, 이 헌법에 의하여 선거방법이나 임명권자가
변경된 공무원과 대법원장 및 감사원장은 이 헌법
에 의하여 후임자가 선임될 때까지 그 직무를 행하
며, 이 경우 전임자인 공무원의 임기는 후임자가 선

임되는 전일까지로 한다.

② 이 헌법시행 당시의 대법원장과 대법원판사가 아닌 법관은 제1항 단서의 규정에 불구하고 이 헌법에 의하여 임명된 것으로 본다.

③ 이 헌법 중 공무원의 임기 또는 중임제한에 관한 규정은 이 헌법에 의하여 그 공무원이 최초로 선출 또는 임명된 때로부터 적용한다.

제5조

이 헌법시행 당시의 법령과 조약은 이 헌법에 위배되지 아니하는 한 그 효력을 지속한다.

제6조

이 헌법시행 당시에 이 헌법에 의하여 새로 설치될 기관의 권한에 속하는 직무를 행하고 있는 기관은 이 헌법에 의하여 새로운 기관이 설치될 때까지 존속하며 그 직무를 행한다.

[헌법 제10호, 1987.10.29.]

제 2 부

CONSTITUTION OF
REPUBLIC OF KOREA

CONSTITUTION OF THE REPUBLIC OF KOREA

Amended by Constitution No. 10, October 29, 1987

PREAMBLE

We, the people of Korea, proud of a resplendent history and traditions dating from time immemorial, upholding the cause of the Provisional Republic of Korea Government born of the March First Independence Movement of 1919 and the democratic ideals of the April Nineteenth Uprising of 1960 against injustice, having assumed the mission of democratic reform and peaceful unification of our homeland and having determined to consolidate national unity with justice, humanitarianism and brotherly love, and to destroy all social vices and injustice, and to afford equal opportunities to every person and provide for the fullest development of individual capabilities in all fields, including political, economic, social, and cultural life by further strengthening the basic free and democratic order conducive to private initiative and public harmony, and to help each person discharge those duties and responsibilities concomitant to freedoms and rights, and to elevate the quality of life for all citizens and contribute to lasting world peace and the common prosperity of mankind and thereby to ensure security, liberty, and happiness for ourselves and our posterity forever, do hereby amend, through national referendum following a resolution by the National Assembly, the Constitution, ordained and established on the Twelfth Day of July anno Domini Nineteen hundred and forty-eight, and amended eight times subsequently. Oct. 29, 1987

CHAPTER I

GENERAL PROVISIONS

Article 1

(1) The Republic of Korea shall be a democratic republic.

(2) The sovereignty of the Republic of Korea shall reside in the people and all state authority shall emanate from the people.

Article 2

(1) Nationality of the people of the Republic of Korea

shall be prescribed by Act.

(2) It shall be the duty of the State to protect citizens residing abroad as prescribed by Act.

Article 3

The territory of the Republic of Korea shall consist of the Korean peninsula and its adjacent islands.

Article 4

The Republic of Korea shall seek unification and shall formulate and carry out a policy of peaceful unification based on the principles of freedom and democracy.

Article 5

(1) The Republic of Korea shall endeavor to maintain international peace and shall renounce all aggressive wars.

(2) The Armed Forces shall be charged with the sacred mission of national security and defense of the land

and their political neutrality shall be maintained.

Article 6

(1) Treaties duly concluded and promulgated under the Constitution and the generally recognized rules of international law shall have the same effect as the domestic laws of the Republic of Korea.

(2) The status of aliens shall be guaranteed as prescribed by international law and treaties.

Article 7

(1) All public officials shall be servants of the people and shall be responsible to the people.

(2) The status and political impartiality of public officials shall be guaranteed as prescribed by Act.

Article 8

(1) The establishment of political parties shall be free and the plural party system shall be guaranteed.

(2) Political parties shall be democratic in their objectives, organization, and activities and shall have the necessary organizational arrangements for the people to participate in the formation of the political will.

(3) Political parties shall enjoy the protection of the State and may be provided with operational funds by the State under the conditions as prescribed by Act.

(4) If the purposes or activities of a political party are contrary to the fundamental democratic order, the Government may bring an action against it in the Constitutional Court for its dissolution, and the political party shall be dissolved in accordance with the decision of the Constitutional Court.

Article 9

The State shall strive to sustain and develop its cultural heritage and to enhance its national culture.

CHAPTER II

RIGHTS AND DUTIES OF CITIZENS

Article 10

All citizens shall be assured of their human worth and dignity and shall have the right to pursue happiness. It shall be the duty of the State to confirm and guarantee the fundamental and inviolable human rights of individuals.

Article 11

(1) All citizens shall be equal before the law and there

shall be no discrimination in political, economic, social, or cultural life on account of sex, religion, or social status.

(2) No privileged caste shall be recognized nor established in any form.

(3) The awarding of decorations or distinctions of honor in any form shall be effective only for recipients and no privileges shall ensue therefrom.

Article 12

(1) All citizens shall enjoy personal liberty. No person shall be arrested, detained, searched, seized, or interrogated except as provided by Act. No person shall be punished, placed under preventive restrictions or be subjected to involuntary labor except as provided by Act and through lawful procedures.

(2) No citizen shall be tortured or be compelled to testify against himself in criminal cases.

(3) Warrants issued by a judge through due procedures upon the request of a prosecutor shall be presented in case of arrest, detention, seizure or search. Provided, that in a case where a criminal suspect is apprehended while in the very act of committing an offense or where there is danger that a person suspected of committing a crime punishable by imprisonment of three years or more may escape or destroy evidence, then investigative authorities may request an ex post facto warrant.

(4) Any person who is arrested or detained shall have the right to prompt assistance of counsel. When a criminal defendant is unable to secure counsel by his own efforts, the State shall assign counsel for the defendant as prescribed by Act.

(5) No person shall be arrested or detained without being informed of the reason thereof and of his right to assistance of counsel. The family, etc., as designated by Act, of a person arrested or detained

shall be notified without delay of the reason for and the time and place of the arrest or detention.

(6) Any person who is arrested or detained shall have the right to request the court to review the legality of the arrest or detention.

(7) In a case where a confession is deemed to have been made against the will of a defendant due to torture, violence, intimidation, unduly prolonged arrest, deceit or in a case where a confession is the only evidence against a defendant in a formal trial, such a confession shall not be admitted as evidence of guilt, nor shall a defendant be punished by reason of such a confession.

Article 13

(1) No citizen shall be prosecuted for an act which does not constitute a crime under an Act in force at the time it was committed, nor shall he be placed in double jeopardy.

(2) No restriction shall be imposed upon the political rights of any citizen, nor shall any person be deprived of property rights by means of retroactive legislation.

(3) No citizen shall suffer unfavorable treatment on account of an act not of his own doing but committed by a relative.

Article 14

All citizens shall enjoy freedom of residence and the right to move at will.

Article 15

All citizens shall enjoy freedom of occupation.

Article 16

All citizens shall be free from intrusion into their place of residence. In case of search or seizure in a residence, a warrant issued by a judge upon request of a prosecutor shall be presented.

Article 17

The right to privacy of all citizens shall not be infringed.

Article 18

The privacy of correspondence of all citizens shall not be infringed.

Article 19

All citizens shall enjoy freedom of conscience.

Article 20

(1) All citizens shall enjoy freedom of religion.

(2) No state religion shall be recognized and there should be a separation of the state and of religion.

Article 21

(1) All citizens shall enjoy the freedom of speech and of the press and the freedom of assembly and of association.

(2) Licensing or censorship of speech and the press and licensing of assembly and association shall not be recognized.

(3) The standards of news service and broadcast facilities and matters necessary to ensure the functions of newspapers shall be determined by Act.

(4) Neither speech nor the press shall violate the honor or rights of other persons nor undermine public morals or social ethics. Should speech or the press violate the honor or rights of other persons, claims may be made for the damage resulting therefrom.

Article 22

(1) All citizens shall enjoy the freedom of learning and

the arts.

(2) The rights of authors, inventors, scientists, engineers, and artists shall be protected by Act.

Article 23

(1) The right of property of all citizens shall be guaranteed. The contents and limitations thereof shall be determined by Act.

(2) The exercise of property rights shall conform to the public welfare.

(3) Expropriation, use or restriction of private property from public necessity and compensation there for shall be governed by Act. Provided, that in such a case, just compensation shall be paid.

Article 24

All citizens shall have the right to vote under the conditions as prescribed by Act.

Article 25

All citizens shall have the right to hold public office under the conditions as prescribed by Act.

Article 26

(1) All citizens shall have the right to petition in writing to any governmental agency under the conditions as prescribed by Act.

(2) The State shall be obligated to examine all such petitions.

Article 27

(1) All citizens shall have the right to be tried in conformity with the Act by judges qualified under the Constitution and the Act.

(2) Citizens who are not on active military service or who are not employees of the military forces shall not be tried by a court martial within the territory of the Republic of Korea, except in case of crimes

as prescribed by Act involving important classified military information, sentinels, sentry posts, the supply of harmful food and beverages, prisoners of war and military Articles and facilities and in the case of a proclamation of extraordinary martial law.

(3) All citizens shall have the right to a speedy trial. The accused shall have the right to a public trial without delay in the absence of justifiable reasons to the contrary.

(4) The accused shall be presumed innocent until a judgment of guilt has been pronounced.

(5) A victim of a crime shall be entitled to make a statement during the proceedings of the trial of the case involved as under the conditions prescribed by Act.

Article 28

In a case where a criminal suspect or an accused person who has been placed under detention is not indicted as provided by Act or is acquitted by a court, he shall be entitled to claim just compensation from the State under the conditions as prescribed by Act.

Article 29

(1) In case a person has sustained damages by an unlawful act committed by a public official in the course of official duties, he may claim just compensation from the State or public organization under the conditions as prescribed by Act. In this case, the public official concerned shall not be immune from liabilities.

(2) In case a person on active military service, an employee of the military forces, a police official, or others as prescribed by Act sustains damages in connection with the performance of official duties such as combat action, drill and so forth, he shall not be entitled to a claim against the State or public organization on the ground of unlawful

acts committed by public officials in the course of official duties, but shall be entitled only to compensations as prescribed by Act.

Article 30

Citizens who have suffered bodily injury or death due to criminal acts of others may receive aid from the State under the conditions as prescribed by Act.

Article 31

(1) All citizens shall have an equal right to receive an education corresponding to their abilities.

(2) All citizens who have children to support shall be responsible at least for their elementary education and other education as provided by Act.

(3) Compulsory education shall be free of charge.

(4) Independence, professionalism, and political impartiality of education and the autonomy of institutions of higher learning shall be guaranteed

under the conditions as prescribed by Act.

(5) The State shall promote lifelong education.

(6) Fundamental matters pertaining to the educational system, including in-school and lifelong education, administration, finance, and the status of teachers shall be determined by Act.

Article 32

(1) All citizens shall have the right to work. The State shall endeavor to promote the employment of workers and to guarantee optimum wages through social and economic means and shall enforce a minimum wage system under the conditions as prescribed by Act.

(2) All citizens shall have the duty to work. The State shall prescribe by Act the extent and conditions of the duty to work in conformity with democratic principles.

(3) Standards of working conditions shall be

determined by Act in such a way as to guarantee human dignity.

(4) Special protection shall be accorded to working women and they shall not be subjected to unjust discrimination in terms of employment, wages, and working conditions.

(5) Special protection shall be accorded to working children.

(6) The opportunity to work shall be accorded preferentially, under the conditions as prescribed by Act, to those who have given distinguished service to the State, wounded veterans and policemen, and members of the bereaved families of military servicemen and policemen killed in action.

Article 33

(1) To enhance working conditions, workers shall have the right to independent association, collective bargaining, and collective action.

(2) Only those public officials, who are designated by Act, shall have the right to association, collective bargaining, and collective action.

(3) The right to collective action of workers employed by important defense industries may be either restricted or denied under the conditions as prescribed by Act.

Article 34

(1) All citizens shall be entitled to a life worthy of human beings.

(2) The State shall have the duty to endeavor to promote social security and welfare.

(3) The State shall endeavor to promote the welfare and rights of women.

(4) The State shall have the duty to implement policies for enhancing the welfare of senior citizens and the minors.

(5) Citizens who are incapable of earning a livelihood

due to a physical disability, disease, old age, or other reasons shall be protected by the State under the conditions as prescribed by Act.

(6) The State shall endeavor to prevent disasters and to protect citizens from harm therefrom.

Article 35

(1) All citizens shall have the right to a healthy and pleasant environment. The State and all citizens shall endeavor to protect the environment.

(2) The substance of the environmental right shall be determined by Act.

(3) The State shall endeavor to ensure comfortable housing for all citizens through housing development policies and the like.

Article 36

(1) Marriage and family life shall be entered into and sustained on the basis of individual dignity

and equality of the sexes, and the State shall do everything in its power to achieve that goal.

(2) The State shall endeavor to protect mothers.

(3) The health of all citizens shall be protected by the State.

Article 37

(1) Freedoms and rights of citizens shall not be neglected on the ground that they are not enumerated in the Constitution.

(2) The freedoms and rights of citizens may be restricted by Act only when necessary for national security, the maintenance of law and order, or for public welfare. Even when such restriction is imposed, no essential aspect of the freedom or right shall be violated.

Article 38

All citizens shall have the duty to pay taxes under the

conditions as prescribed by Act.

Article 39

(1) All citizens shall have the duty of national defense under the conditions as prescribed by Act.

(2) No citizen shall be treated unfavorably on account of the fulfillment of his obligation of military service.

CHAPTER III

THE NATIONAL ASSEMBLY

Article 40

The legislative power shall be vested in the National Assembly.

Article 41

(1) The National Assembly shall be composed of members elected by universal, equal, direct, and secret ballot by the citizens.

(2) The number of members of the National Assembly

shall be determined by Act, but the number shall not be less than 200.

(3) The constituencies of members of the National Assembly, proportional representation, and other matters pertaining to National Assembly elections shall be determined by Act.

Article 42

The term of office of members of the National Assembly shall be four years.

Article 43

Members of the National Assembly shall not concurrently hold any other office prescribed by Act.

Article 44

(1) During the sessions of the National Assembly, no member of the National Assembly shall be arrested or detained without the consent of the National

Assembly except in case the member is in the very act of committing an offense.

(2) In case of apprehension or detention of a member of the National Assembly prior to the opening of a session, such member shall be released during the session upon the request of the National Assembly, except when the member is apprehended and detained while in the very act of committing an offense.

Article 45

No member of the National Assembly shall be held responsible outside the National Assembly for opinions officially expressed or votes cast in the Assembly.

Article 46

(1) Members of the National Assembly shall have the duty to maintain high standards of integrity.

(2) Members of the National Assembly shall give

preference to national interests and shall perform their duties in accordance with their conscience.

(3) Members of the National Assembly shall not acquire, through abuse of their positions, rights, and interests in property or positions, or assist other persons to acquire the same, by means of contracts with or dispositions by the State, public organizations, or industries.

Article 47

(1) A regular session of the National Assembly shall be convened once every year under the conditions as prescribed by Act and extraordinary sessions of the National Assembly shall be convened upon the request of the President or one fourth or more of the total members.

(2) The period of regular sessions shall not exceed a hundred days, and that of extraordinary sessions, thirty days.

(3) If the President requests the convening of an extraordinary session, the period of the session and the reasons for the request shall be clearly specified.

Article 48

The National Assembly shall elect one Speaker and two Vice-Speakers.

Article 49

Except as otherwise provided for in the Constitution or in Act, the attendance of a majority of the total members, and the concurrent vote of a majority of the members present, shall be necessary for decisions of the National Assembly. In case of a tie vote, the matter shall be regarded as rejected.

Article 50

(1) Sessions of the National Assembly shall be open to the public. Provided, that when it is decided so

by a majority of the members present or when the Speaker deems it necessary to do so for the sake of national security, they may be closed to the public.

(2) The public disclosure of the proceedings of sessions which were not open to the public shall be determined by Act.

Article 51

Bills and other matters submitted to the National Assembly for deliberation shall not be abandoned on the ground that they were not acted upon during the session in which they were introduced, except in a case where the term of the members of the National Assembly has expired.

Article 52

Bills may be introduced by members of the National Assembly or by the Executive.

Article 53

(1) Each bill passed by the National Assembly shall be sent to the Executive, and the President shall promulgate it within fifteen days.

(2) In case of objection to a bill, the President may, within the period referred to in paragraph (1), return it to the National Assembly with written explanation of his objection, and request it be reconsidered. The President may do the same during adjournment of the National Assembly.

(3) The President shall not request the National Assembly to reconsider a bill in part, or with proposed amendments.

(4) In case there is a request for reconsideration of a bill, the National Assembly shall reconsider it, and if the National Assembly again passes the bill in the original form with the attendance of more than one half of the total members, and with a concurrent vote of two thirds or more of the

members present, it shall become Act.

(5) If the President does not promulgate a bill, or does not request the National Assembly to reconsider it within the period referred to in paragraph (1), it shall become Act.

(6) The President shall promulgate without delay an Act as finalized under paragraphs (4) and (5). If the President does not promulgate an Act within five days after it has become Act under paragraph (5), or after it has been returned to the Executive under paragraph (4), the Speaker shall promulgate it.

(7) Except as provided otherwise, an Act shall take effect twenty days after the date of promulgation.

Article 54

(1) The National Assembly shall deliberate and decide upon the national budget bill.

(2) The Executive shall formulate the budget bill for each fiscal year and submit it to the National

Assembly within ninety days before the beginning of a fiscal year. The National Assembly shall decide upon it within thirty days before the beginning of the fiscal year.

(3) If the budget bill is not passed by the beginning of the fiscal year, the Executive may, in conformity with the budget of the previous fiscal year, disburse funds for the following purposes until the budget bill is passed by the National Assembly:

1. The maintenance and operation of agencies and facilities established by the Constitution or by Act

2. Execution of the obligatory expenditures as prescribed by Act

3. Continuation of projects previously approved in the budget.

Article 55

(1) In a case where it is necessary to make continuing

disbursements for a period longer than one fiscal year, the Executive shall obtain the approval of the National Assembly for a specified period of time.

(2) A reserve fund shall be approved by the National Assembly in its totality. The disbursement of the reserve fund shall be approved during the next session of the National Assembly.

Article 56

When it is necessary to amend the budget, the Executive may formulate a supplementary revised budget bill and submit it to the National Assembly.

Article 57

The National Assembly shall not, without the consent of the Executive, increase the sum of any item of expenditure or create any new items of expenditure in the budget submitted by the Executive.

Article 58

When the Executive plans to issue national bonds or to conclude contracts which may incur financial obligations on the State outside the budget, it shall have the prior concurrence of the National Assembly.

Article 59

Types and rates of taxes shall be determined by Act.

Article 60

(1) The National Assembly shall have the right to consent to the conclusion and ratification of treaties pertaining to mutual assistance or mutual security; treaties concerning important international organizations; treaties of friendship, trade, and navigation; treaties pertaining to any restriction in sovereignty; peace treaties; treaties which will burden the State or people with an important financial obligation; or treaties related to legislative matters.

(2) The National Assembly shall also have the right to consent to the declaration of war, the dispatch of armed forces to foreign states, or the stationing of alien forces in the territory of the Republic of Korea.

Article 61

(1) The National Assembly may inspect affairs of the state or investigate specific matters of state affairs and may demand the production of documents directly related thereto, the appearance of a witness in person, and the furnishing of testimony or statements of opinion.

(2) The procedures and other necessary matters concerning the inspection and investigation of state administration shall be determined by Act.

Article 62

(1) The Prime Minister, members of the State Council,

or government delegates may attend meetings of the National Assembly or its committees and report on the state administration or deliver opinions and answer questions.

(2) When requested by the National Assembly or its committees, the Prime Minister, members of the State Council or government delegates shall attend any meeting of the National Assembly and answer questions. If the Prime Minister or State Council members are requested to attend, the Prime Minister or State Council members may have State Council members or government delegates attend any meeting of the National Assembly and answer questions.

Article 63

(1) The National Assembly may pass a recommendation for the removal of the Prime Minister or a State Council member from office.

(2) A recommendation for removal as referred to in paragraph (1) may be introduced by one third or more of the total members of the National Assembly, and shall be passed with the concurrent vote of a majority of the total members of the National Assembly.

Article 64

(1) The National Assembly may establish the rules of its proceedings and internal regulations. Provided, that they are not in conflict with an Act.

(2) The National Assembly may review the qualifications of its members and may take disciplinary actions against its members.

(3) The concurrent vote of two thirds or more of the total members of the National Assembly shall be required for the expulsion of any member.

(4) No action shall be brought to court with regard to decisions taken under paragraphs (2) and (3).

Article 65

(1) In case the President, the Prime Minister, members of the State Council, heads of Executive Ministries, Justices of the Constitutional Court, judges, members of the National Election Commission, the Chairman and members of the Board of Audit and Inspection, and other public officials designated by Act have violated the Constitution or other Acts in the performance of official duties, the National Assembly may pass motions for their impeachment.

(2) A motion for impeachment prescribed in paragraph (1) may be proposed by one third or more of the total members of the National Assembly, and shall require a concurrent vote of a majority of the total members of the National Assembly for passage. Provided, that a motion for the impeachment of the President shall be proposed by a majority of the total members of the National Assembly and approved by two thirds or more of the total

members of the National Assembly.

(3) Any person against whom a motion for impeachment has been passed shall be suspended from exercising his power until the impeachment has been adjudicated.

(4) A decision on impeachment shall not extend further than removal from public office. Provided, that it shall not exempt the person impeached from civil or criminal liability.

CHAPTER IV

THE EXECUTIVE

SECTION 1.

The President

Article 66

(1) The President shall be the Head of State and shall represent the State vis-a-vis foreign states.

(2) The President shall have the responsibility and duty to safeguard the independence, territorial integrity, and continuity of the State and the

Constitution.

(3) The President shall have the duty to sincerely pursue the peaceful unification of the homeland.

(4) Executive power shall be vested in the Executive Branch headed by the President.

Article 67

(1) The President shall be elected by universal, equal, direct, and secret ballot by the people.

(2) In case two or more persons receive the same largest number of votes in the election as referred to in paragraph (1), the person who receives the largest number of votes in an open session of the National Assembly attended by a majority of the total members of the National Assembly shall be elected.

(3) If and when there is only one presidential candidate, he shall not be elected President unless he receives at least one third of the total eligible

votes.

(4) Citizens who are eligible for election to the National Assembly, and who have reached the age of forty years or more on the date of the presidential election, shall be eligible to be elected to the presidency.

(5) Matters pertaining to presidential elections shall be determined by Act.

Article 68

(1) The successor to the incumbent President shall be elected forty to seventy days before his term expires.

(2) In case a vacancy occurs in the office of the President, or the President-elect dies, or is disqualified by a court ruling or for any other reason, a successor shall be elected within sixty days from the date when the vacancy, death, or disqualification occurs.

Article 69

The President, at the time of his inauguration, shall take the following oath: "I do solemnly swear before the people that I will faithfully execute the duties of the President by observing the Constitution, defending the State, pursuing the peaceful unification of the homeland, promoting the freedom and welfare of the people and endeavoring to develop national culture."

Article 70

The term of the office of the President shall be five years, without reelection.

Article 71

If the Office of the President is vacant or the President is unable to perform his duties for any reason, the Prime Minister or the members of the State Council in the orderof priority as determined by Act, shall act for him.

Article 72

The President may submit important policies relating to diplomacy, national defense, unification, and other matters relating to the national destiny to a national referendum if he deems it necessary.

Article 73

The President shall conclude and ratify treaties; accredit, receive or dispatch diplomatic envoys; and declare war and conclude peace.

Article 74

(1) The President shall be Commander-in-Chief of the Armed Forces under the conditions as prescribed by the Constitution and by Act.

(2) The organization and formation of the Armed Forces shall be determined by Act.

Article 75

The President may issue presidential decrees concerning matters delegated to him by Act with the scope specifically defined and also matters necessary to enforce Acts.

Article 76

(1) In time of internal turmoil, external menace, natural calamity, or a grave financial or economic crisis, the President may take the minimum necessary financial and economic actions or issue orders having the effect of Act, only when it is required to take urgent measures for the maintenance of national security or public peace and order, and there is no time to await the convocation of the National Assembly.

(2) In case of major hostilities affecting national security, the President may issue orders having the effect of Act, only when it is required to preserve

the integrity of the nation, and it is impossible to convene the National Assembly.

(3) In case actions taken or orders issued under paragraphs (1) and (2), the President shall promptly notify the National Assembly and obtain its approval.

(4) In case no approval is obtained, the actions or orders shall lose its effect. In such case, the Acts which were amended or abolished by the orders in question shall automatically regain their original effect from the moment the orders fail to obtain approval.

(5) The President shall, without delay, make public notice developments under paragraphs (3) and (4).

Article 77

(1) When the President required to cope with a military necessity or to maintain the public safety and order by mobilization of the military forces

in time of war, armed conflict, or similar national emergency, he may proclaim martial law under the conditions as prescribed by Act.

(2) Martial law shall be of two types: extraordinary martial law and precautionary martial law.

(3) Under extraordinary martial law, special measures may be taken with respect to the necessity for warrants, freedom of speech, the press, assembly and association, or the powers of the Executive and the Judiciary under the conditions as prescribed by Act.

(4) When the President has proclaimed martial law, he shall notify the National Assembly without delay.

(5) When the National Assembly requests the lifting of martial law with the concurrent vote of a majority of the total members of the National Assembly, the President shall comply.

Article 78

The President shall appoint and dismiss public officials under the conditions as prescribed by the Constitution and by Act.

Article 79

(1) The President may grant amnesty, commutation, and restoration of rights under the conditions as prescribed by Act.

(2) The President shall receive the consent of the National Assembly in granting a general amnesty.

(3) Matters pertaining to amnesty, commutation, and restoration of rights shall be determined by Act.

Article 80

The President shall award decorations and other honors under the conditions as prescribed by Act.

Article 81

The President may appear before and address the National Assembly or express his views by written message.

Article 82

The acts of the President under law shall be executed in writing, and such documents shall be countersigned by the Prime Minister and the members of the State Council concerned. The same shall apply to military affairs.

Article 83

The President shall not concurrently hold the office of Prime Minister, a membership 62 Ministry of Government Legislation in the State Council, the head of any Executive Ministry, nor other public or private posts as prescribed by Act.

Article 84

The President shall not be charged with a criminal offense during his tenure of office except for insurrection or treason.

Article 85

Matters pertaining to the status and courteous treatment of former Presidents shall be determined by Act.

SECTION 2.

The Executive Branch

Sub-Section 1.

The Prime Minister and Members of the State Council

Article 86

(1) The Prime Minister shall be appointed by the

President with the consent of the National Assembly.

(2) The Prime Minister shall assist the President and shall direct the Executive Ministries under order of the President.

(3) No member of the military shall be appointed Prime Minister unless he is retired from active duty.

Article 87

(1) The members of the State Council shall be appointed by the President on the recommendation of the Prime Minister.

(2) The members of the State Council shall assist the President in the conduct of State affairs and as constituents of the State Council, shall deliberate on State affairs.

(3) The Prime Minister may recommend to the President the removal of a member of the State

Council from office.

(4) No member of the military shall be appointed a member of the State Council unless he is retired from active duty.

Sub−Section 2.

The State Council

Article 88

(1) The State Council shall deliberate on important policies that fall within the power of the Executive.

(2) The State Council shall be composed of the President, the Prime Minister, and other members whose number shall not be more than thirty and not less than fifteen.

(3) The President shall be the chairman of the State Council, and the Prime Minister shall be the Vice−Chairman.

Article 89

The following matters shall be referred to the State Council for deliberation:

1. Basic plans for state affairs and general policies of the Executive

2. Declaration of war, conclusion of peace, and other important matters pertaining to foreign policy

3. Draft amendments to the Constitution, proposals for national referendums, proposed treaties, legislative bills, and proposed presidential decrees

4. Budgets, settlement of accounts, basic plans for disposal of state properties, contracts incurring financial obligation on the State, and other important financial matters

5. Emergency orders and emergency financial and economic actions or orders by the President, and declaration and termination of martial law

6. Important military affairs

7. Requests for convening an extraordinary session of

the National Assembly

8. Awarding of honors

9. Granting of amnesty, commutation, and restoration of rights

10. Demarcation of jurisdiction between Executive Ministries

11. Basic plans concerning delegation or allocation of powers within the Executive

12. Evaluation and analysis of the administration of State affairs

13. Formulation and coordination of important policies of each Executive Ministry

14. Action for the dissolution of a political party

15. Examination of petitions pertaining to executive policies submitted or referred to the Executive

16. Appointment of the Prosecutor General, the Chairman of the Joint Chiefs of Staff, the Chief of Staff of each armed service, the presidents of national universities, ambassadors, and such other

public officials and managers of important State-run enterprises as designated by Act

17. Other matters presented by the President, the Prime Minister or a member of the State Council.

Article 90

(1) An Advisory Council of Elder Statesmen, composed of elder statesmen, may be established to advise the President on important affairs of State.

(2) The immediate former President shall become the Chairman of the Advisory Council of Elder Statesmen. Provided, that if there is no immediate former President, the President shall appoint the Chairman.

(3) The organization, function, and other necessary matters pertaining to the Advisory Council of Elder Statesmen shall be determined by Act.

Article 91

(1) A National Security Council shall be established to advise the President on the formulation of foreign, military, and domestic policies related to national security prior to their deliberation by the State Council.

(2) The meetings of the National Security Council shall be presided over by the President.

(3) The organization, function, and other necessary matters pertaining to the National Security Council shall be determined by Act.

Article 92

(1) An Advisory Council on Democratic and Peaceful Unification may be established to advise the President on the formulation of peaceful unification policies.

(2) The organization, function, and other necessary matters pertaining to the Advisory Council on

Democratic and Peaceful Unification shall be
determined by Act.

Article 93

(1) A National Economic Advisory Council may
be established to advise the President on the
formulation of important policies for developing
the national economy.

(2) The organization, function, and other necessary
matters pertaining to the National Laws on Green
Growth, and Economic Investment in Korea 65
Economic Advisory Council shall be determined by
Act.

Sub–Section 3.

The Executive Ministries

Article 94

Heads of Executive Ministries shall be appointed by the President from among members of the State Council on the recommendation of the Prime Minister.

Article 95

The Prime Minister or the head of each Executive Ministry may, under the powers delegated by Act or Presidential Decree or ex officio, issue ordinances of the Prime Minister or the Executive Ministry concerning matters that are within their jurisdiction.

Article 96

The establishment, organization, and function of each Executive Ministry shall be determined by Act.

Sub-Section 4.

The Board of Audit and Inspection

Article 97

The Board of Audit and Inspection shall be established under the direct supervision of the President to inspect and examine the settlement of the revenues and expenditures of the State, the accounts of the State and other organizations specified by Act and the job performances of the executive agencies and public officials.

Article 98

(1) The Board of Audit and Inspection shall be composed of not less than five and not more than eleven members, including the Chairman.

(2) The Chairman of the Board shall be appointed by the President with the consent of the National Assembly. The term of office of the Chairman shall

be four years and he may be reappointed only once.

(3) The members of the Board shall be appointed by the President on the recommendation of the Chairman. The term of office of the members shall be four years and they may be reappointed only once.

Article 99

The Board of Audit and Inspection shall inspect the closing of accounts of revenues and expenditures each year and report the results to the President and the National Assembly in the following year.

Article 100

The organization and function of the Board of Audit and Inspection, the qualifications of its members, the range of the public officials subject to inspection, and other necessary matters shall be determined by Act.

CHAPTER V

THE COURTS

Article 101

(1) Judicial power shall be vested in courts composed of judges.

(2) The courts shall be composed of the Supreme Court, which is the highest court of the State, and other courts at specified levels.

(3) Qualifications for judges shall be determined by Act.

Article 102

(1) Departments may be established in the Supreme Court.

(2) There shall be Supreme Court Justices at the Supreme Court. Provided, that judges other than Supreme Court Justices may be assigned to the Supreme Court under the conditions as prescribed by Act.

(3) The organization of the Supreme Court and lower courts shall be determined by Act.

Article 103

Judges shall rule independently according to their conscience and in conformity with the Constitution and laws.

Article 104

(1) The Chief Justice of the Supreme Court shall be appointed by the President with the consent of the

National Assembly.

(2) The Supreme Court Justices shall be appointed by the President on the recommendation of the Chief Justice and with the consent of the National Assembly.

(3) Judges other than the Chief Justice and the Supreme Court Justices shall be appointed by the Chief Justice with the consent of the Conference of Supreme Court Justices.

Article 105

(1) The term of office of the Chief justice shall be six years, without reappointment.

(2) The term of office of the Justices of the Supreme Court shall be six years and they may be reappointed as prescribed by Act.

(3) The term of office of judges other than the Chief Justice and Justices of the Supreme Court shall be ten years and they may be reappointed under the

conditions as prescribed by Act.

(4) The retirement age of judges shall be determined by Act.

Article 106

(1) No judge shall be removed from office except by impeachment or a sentence of imprisonment without prison labor or heavier punishment, nor shall he be suspended from office, have his salary reduced, or suffer any other unfavorable treatment except by disciplinary action.

(2) In the event a judge is unable to discharge his official duties because of serious mental or physical impairment, he may be retired from office under the conditions as prescribed by Act.

Article 107

(1) When the constitutionality of a law is at issue in a trial, the court shall request a decision of the

Constitutional Court, and shall judge according to the decision thereof.

(2) The Supreme Court shall have the power to make a final review of the constitutionality or legality of administrative decrees, regulations or actions, when their constitutionality or legality is at issue in a trial.

(3) Administrative appeals may be conducted as a procedure prior to a judicial trial. The procedure of administrative appeals shall be determined by Act and shall be in conformity with the principles of judicial procedures.

Article 108

The Supreme Court may establish, within the scope of an Act, regulations pertaining to judicial proceedings and internal discipline and regulations on administrative matters of the court.

Article 109

Trials and decisions of the courts shall be open to the public. Provided, that when there is a danger that such trials may undermine the national security or disturb public safety and order, or be harmful to public morals, trials may be closed to the public by court decision.

Article 110

(1) Courts-martial may be established as special courts to exercise jurisdiction over military trials.

(2) The Supreme Court shall have the final appellate jurisdiction over courts-martial.

(3) The organization and authority of courts-martial and the qualifications of their judges shall be determined by Act.

(4) Military trials under an extraordinary martial law may not be appealed in case of crimes of soldiers and employees of the military; military espionage; and crimes as defined by Act in regard to sentinels,

sentry posts, supply of harmful foods and beverages, and prisoners of war, except in the case of a death sentence.

CHAPTER VI

THE CONSTITUTIONAL COURT

Article 111

(1) The Constitutional Court shall have jurisdiction over the following matters:

1. The constitutionality of a law upon the request of the courts

2. Impeachment

3. Dissolution of a political party

4. Competence disputes between State agencies, between State agencies and local governments,

and between local governments

5. Constitutional complaint as prescribed by Act

(2) The Constitutional Court shall be composed of nine Justices qualified to be court judges, and they shall be appointed by the President.

(3) Among the Justices referred to in paragraph (2), three shall be appointed from persons selected by the National Assembly, and three shall be appointed from persons nominated by the Chief Justice of the Supreme Court.

(4) The president of the Constitutional Court shall be appointed by the President from among the Justices with the consent of the National Assembly.

Article 112

(1) The term of office of the Justices of the Constitutional Court shall be six years and they may be reappointed under the conditions as prescribed by Act.

(2) The Justices of the Constitutional Court shall not join any political party, nor shall they participate in political activities.

(3) No Justice of the Constitutional Court shall be expelled from office except by impeachment or a sentence of imprisonment without prison labor or heavier punishment.

Article 113

(1) When the Constitutional Court makes a decision on the constitutionality of a law, a decision of impeachment, a decision of dissolution of a political party, or an affirmative decision regarding the constitutional complaint, the concurrence of six Justices or more shall be required.

(2) The Constitutional Court may establish regulations relating to its proceedings and internal discipline and regulations on administrative matters within the limits of Act.

(3) The organization, function, and other necessary matters of the Constitutional Court shall be determined by Act.

CHAPTER VII

ELECTION MANAGEMENT

Article 114

(1) Election commissions shall be established for the purpose of fair management of elections and national referenda, and dealing with administrative affairs concerning political parties.

(2) The National Election Commission shall be composed of three members appointed by the President, three members selected by the National Assembly, and three members designated by the

Chief Justice of the Supreme Court. The Chairman of the Commission shall be elected from among the members.

(3) The term of office of the members of the Commission shall be six years.

(4) The members of the Commission shall not join political parties nor shall they participate in political activities.

(5) No member of the Commission shall be expelled from office except by impeachment or a sentence of imprisonment without prison labor or heavier punishment.

(6) The National Election Commission may establish, within the limit of Acts and decrees, regulations relating to the management of elections, national referenda, and administrative affairs concerning political parties and may also establish regulations relating to internal discipline that are compatible with Act.

(7) The organization, function, and other necessary matters of the election commissions at each level shall be determined by Act.

Article 115

(1) Election commissions at each level may issue necessary instructions to administrative agencies concerned with respect to administrative affairs pertaining to elections and national referenda such as the preparation of the poll books.

(2) Administrative agencies concerned, upon receipt of such instructions, shall comply.

Article 116

(1) Election campaigns shall be conducted under the management of the election commissions at each level within the limit set by Act. Equal opportunity shall be guaranteed.

(2) Except as otherwise prescribed by Act,

expenditures for elections shall not be imposed on political parties or candidates.

CHAPTER VIII

LOCAL AUTONOMY

Article 117

(1) Local governments shall deal with administrative matters pertaining to the welfare of local residents, manage properties, and may enact provisions relating to local autonomy, within the limit of Acts and subordinate statutes.

(2) The types of local governments shall be determined by Act.

Article 118

(1) A local government shall have a council.

(2) The organization and powers of local councils, and the election of members; election procedures for heads of local governments; and other matters pertaining to the organization and operation of local governments shall be determined by Act.

CHAPTER IX

THE ECONOMY

Article 119

(1) The economic order of the Republic of Korea shall be based on a respect for the freedom and creative initiative of enterprises and individuals in economic affairs.

(2) The State may regulate and coordinate economic affairs in order to maintain the balanced growth and stability of the national economy, to ensure proper distribution of income, to prevent the domination

of the market and the abuse of economic power and to democratize the economy through harmony among the economic agents.

Article 120

(1) Licenses to exploit, develop, or utilize minerals and all other important underground resources, marine resources, water power, and natural powers available for economic use may be granted for a period of time under the conditions as prescribed by Act.

(2) The land and natural resources shall be protected by the State, and the State shall establish a plan necessary for their balanced development and utilization.

Article 121

(1) The State shall endeavor to realize the land-to-the-tillers principle with respect to agricultural land. Tenant farming shall be prohibited.

(2) The leasing of agricultural land and the consignment management of agricultural land to increase agricultural productivity and to ensure the rational utilization of agricultural land or due to unavoidable circumstances, shall be recognized under the conditions prescribed by Act.

Article 122

The State may impose, under the conditions prescribed by Act, restrictions or obligations necessary for the efficient and balanced utilization, development, and preservation of the land of the nation that is the basis for the productive activities and daily lives of all citizens.

Article 123

(1) The State shall establish and implement a plan to comprehensively develop and support the farm and fishing communities in order to protect and foster agriculture and fisheries.

(2) The State shall have the duty to foster regional economies to ensure the balanced development of all regions.

(3) The State shall protect and foster small and medium enterprises.

(4) In order to protect the interests of farmers and fishermen, the State shall endeavor to stabilize the prices of agricultural and fishery products by maintaining an equilibrium between the demand and supply of such products and improving their marketing and distribution systems.

(5) The State shall foster organizations founded on the spirit of self-help among farmers, fishermen, and businessmen engaged in small and medium industry and shall guarantee their independent activities and development.

Article 124

The State shall guarantee the consumer protection

movement intended to encourage sound consumption activities and improvement in the quality of products under the conditions as prescribed by Act.

Article 125

The State shall foster foreign trade, and may regulate and coordinate it.

Article 126

Private enterprises shall not be nationalized nor transferred to ownership by a local government, nor shall their management be controlled or administered by the State, except in cases as prescribed by Act, to meet urgent necessities of national defense or the national economy.

Article 127

(1) The State shall strive to develop the national economy by developing science and technology, information and human resources and encouraging

innovation.

(2) The State shall establish a system of national standards.

(3) The President may establish advisory organizations necessary to achieve the purpose referred to in paragraph (1).

CHAPTER X

AMENDMENTS TO THE CONSTITUTION

Article 128

(1) A proposal to amend the Constitution shall be introduced either by a majority of the total members of the National Assembly or by the President.

(2) Amendments to the Constitution for the extension of the term of office of the President or for a change allowing for the reelection of the President shall not be effective for the President in office at the

time of the proposal for such amendments to the Constitution.

Article 129

Proposed amendments to the Constitution shall be put before the public by the President for twenty days or more.

Article 130

(1) The National Assembly shall decide upon the proposed amendments within sixty days of the public announcement, and passage by the National Assembly shall require the concurrent vote of two thirds or more of the total members of the National Assembly.

(2) The proposed amendments to the Constitution shall be submitted to a national referendum not later than thirty days after the passage by the National Assembly, and shall be determined by

more than one half of all votes cast by more than one half of voters eligible to vote in elections for members of the National Assembly.

(3) When the proposed amendments to the Constitution receive the concurrence prescribed in paragraph (2), the amendments to the Constitution shall be finalized, and the President shall promulgate it without delay.

ADDENDA

Article 1

This Constitution shall enter into force on the twenty-fifth day of February, anno Domini Nineteen hundred and eighty-eight. Provided, that the enactment or amendment of Acts necessary to implement this Constitution, the elections of the President and the National Assembly under this Constitution and other preparations to implement this Constitution may be carried out prior to the entry into force of this

Constitution.

Article 2

(1) The first presidential election under this Constitution shall be held not later than forty days before this Constitution enters into force.

(2) The term of office of the first President under this Constitution shall commence on the date of its enforcement.

Article 3

(1) The first elections of the National Assembly under this Constitution shall be held within six months from the promulgation of this Constitution. The term of office of the members of the first National Assembly elected under this Constitution shall commence on the date of the first convening of the National Assembly under this Constitution.

(2) The term of office of the members of the National

Assembly incumbent at the time this Constitution is promulgated shall terminate the day prior to the first convening of the National Assembly under paragraph (1).

Article 4

(1) Public officials and officers of enterprises appointed by the Government, who are in office at the time of the enforcement of this Constitution, shall be considered as having been appointed under this Constitution. Provided, that public officials whose election procedures or appointing authorities are changed under this Constitution, the Chief Justice of the Supreme Court and the Chairman of the Board of Audit and Inspection shall remain in office until such time as their successors are chosen under this Constitution, and their terms of office shall terminate the day before the installation of their successors.

(2) Judges attached to the Supreme Court who is not the Chief Justice, Justices of the Supreme Court, and other judges and justices who are in office at the time of the enforcement of this Constitution shall be considered as having been appointed under this Constitution notwithstanding the proviso of paragraph (1).

(3) Those provisions of this Constitution which prescribe the terms of office of public officials or which restrict the number of terms that public officials may serve, shall take effect upon the dates of the first elections or the first appointments of such public officials under this Constitution.

Article 5

Acts, decrees, ordinances, and treaties in force at the time this Constitution enters into force, shall remain valid unless they are contrary to this Constitution.

Article 6

Those organizations existing at the time of the enforcement of this Constitution which have been performing the functions falling within the authority of new organizations to be created under this Constitution, shall continue to exist and perform such functions until such time as the new organizations are created under this Constitution.

Amended by Constitution No. 10, October 29, 1987

대한민국 헌법

개정판 1쇄 펴낸 날 2024년 5월 30일

지 은 이 대한민국
펴 낸 이 장영재
펴 낸 곳 (주)미르북컴퍼니
자 회 사 더휴먼
전   화 02)3141-4421
팩   스 0505-333-4428
등   록 2012년 3월 16일(제313-2012-81호)
주   소 서울시 마포구 성미산로32길 12, 2층 (우 03983)
E - mail sanhonjinju@naver.com
카   페 cafe.naver.com/mirbookcompany
S N S instagram.com/mirbooks